"Tony Suarez is one of the emerging prophetic voices God is raising up to bring the spirit of revival to the Body of Christ and to the nations. God is using him to minister the power of God to a generation who needs to experience the move of the Holy Spirit in signs and wonders. His latest book, *Defeating the Spirit of Hyena*, is very timely for God's people who are being confronted with a mocking spirit, which is attempting to silence their voices and intimidate them from taking a bold stand in the culture. This book is a must read for every believer who wants to assume their God-ordained role in establishing the Kingdom on earth."

—Hank and Brenda Kunneman
Senior Pastors, Lord of Hosts Church &
One Voice Ministries
Omaha, Nebraska, USA

DEFEATING THE SPIRIT OF HYENA

DEFEATING THE SPIRIT OF HYENA

HOW GOD FIGHTS FOR YOU AND WHAT TO DO ABOUT YOUR ADVERSARY

TONY SUÁREZ

DEFEATING THE SPIRIT OF HYENA
How God Fights for You and What to Do about Your Adversary

Copyright © 2021 Anthony Suárez

Published by Revivalmakers
Nashville, Tennessee, USA
www.tonysuarez.com

No part of this book may be reproduced, stored in a retrieval system or transmitted in any form or by any means—electronic, mechanical, photocopy, recording, or any other—except for brief quotations, without permission in writing from the author.

Scripture quotations marked ESV are from The Holy Bible, English Standard Version. ESV® Text Edition: 2016. Copyright © 2001 by Crossway Bibles, a publishing ministry of Good News Publishers. Scripture quotations marked KJV are taken from the King James Version of the Bible, which is in the public domain. Scripture quotations marked NIV are from the Holy Bible, New International Version®, NIV® Copyright ©1973, 1978, 1984, 2011 by Biblica, Inc.® Used by permission. All rights reserved worldwide. Scripture quotations marked NKJV are taken from the New King James Version®. Copyright © 1982 by Thomas Nelson. Used by permission. All rights reserved. Scripture quotations marked NLT are taken from the Holy Bible, New Living Translation, copyright ©1996, 2004, 2015 by Tyndale House Foundation. Used by permission of Tyndale House Publishers, a Division of Tyndale House Ministries, Carol Stream, Illinois 60188. All rights reserved.

Cover by Shiloh Strobel
Interior by Katherine Lloyd at theDESKonline.com

Printed in the United States of America
21 22 23 24 25 5 4 3 2 1

CONTENTS

Chapter 1　**STATE OF SPIRITUAL CRISIS** 1

Chapter 2　**ENOUGH IS ENOUGH** 7

Chapter 3　**MOCKERS AND THIEVES**. 11

Chapter 4　**KICK THAT DEVIL OUT** 19

Chapter 5　**HOW GOD FIGHTS FOR YOU** 29

35 Victory Scriptures. 43

About the Author. 53

Chapter 1

STATE OF SPIRITUAL CRISIS

As you have observed world events in the last few years, have you thought, *We've never been down this road before* or *We've never lived through anything like this before.*

There is a good reason to think this: from viruses to stranger-than-normal election cycles to public unrest. Humanity, however, tends to have a short-term memory, especially when it comes to living through difficult times. I'm guilty of using these phrases, but the Holy Spirit recently arrested my thoughts and said, "Oh, really? Humanity has never had it worse? Pause and think, *Is this really the worst of times?*"

A simple history study of the last two centuries reveals that a decade hasn't gone by without war, pandemics, economic crisis, ethnic tension, and so on. In fact, so much has happened that it seems we've forgotten the trials and difficulties of old, and more importantly how God made a way of healing, deliverance, and salvation for us!

With that being said, I do find the spiritual state of our world in crisis. The level of spiritual warfare is unprecedented. Our children are fighting demonic powers and influences that, in my opinion, previous generations did not have to wrestle with, or at least not to this level. I'm speaking specifically to the evil forces of perversion and rebellion plaguing our land.

If the enemy has saved some of his best artillery for the last hour, it's because he understands how crucial this hour is.

This is the hour of revival.

This is the hour of the final harvest.

This is the church's finest hour.

The enemy is stopping at nothing to try and prevent these three statements from being true. While we have lived through wars, pandemics, economic crisis, and such in previous generations, I do not believe any generation has lived through this level of mockery, attack, criticism, and outright disrespect for the things of God.

If the enemy has saved some of his best artillery for the last hour, it's because he understands how crucial this hour is.

When I think of what's considered the good ol' days of Americana, I think of the traditional family, picket fences, family BBQs, kids' baseball on Saturday, church on Sunday, Easter photos, and holiday celebrations. I think of wholesome television specials that the entire family could gather and watch together without having to sort through foul language and sexual immorality. I think of parents rearing their children toward success, and children respecting not only their parents but all authority.

Yes, those good ol' days seem gone. Believing, modeling, and striving for a traditional family is now controversial. Teaching children that there are only two genders and God picks which one you are is considered abusive. Forcing your children to attend church or read the Bible is considered extreme. The sad reality is that it wasn't so long ago that these customs and truths were normal ... even outside of Christian circles.

We are living with the repercussions of the decisions of yesteryear ... removing prayer from school, accepting teachings contrary to Scripture (such as evolution), and removing landmarks of our faith. This has led to a faithless generation that makes mockery rather than has reverence for the holy things of God.

The blame, though, for how we got here cannot simply be laid at the feet of unbelievers. The church is culpable as well. The church that was born with tongues of fire in Acts has had some of its own "church kids" try to put the fire out in the last several decades. We've lessened how much we gather as a body of believers, and we now have leaders opining that in-person gatherings aren't that important at all!

Wells of truth have become polluted with sensationalism and falsehoods to the degree that rather than clean polluted wells, the sons of the church capped them off. With that, a generation has risen that does not know the fire of God, the power of consecration, or the promises of the word of faith, abundance, healing, and favor like previous generations did.

This outlook can be overwhelmingly discouraging, but I promise that before you finish this book, you will be encouraged. This is a season of victory. But to obtain victory we must identify our enemy! That's what we're doing right now. We're exposing our enemy, his strategies, and his lies!

A generation has risen that does not know the fire of God, the power of consecration, or the promises of the word of faith, abundance, healing, and favor.

Chapter 2

ENOUGH IS ENOUGH

Isaiah 63 (NLT) opens with the prophet asking:

> Who is this who comes from Edom, from the city of Bozrah, with his clothing stained red? Who is this in royal robes, marching in his great strength?

To which a response comes from heaven saying:

> "It is I, the LORD, announcing your salvation! It is I, the LORD, who has the power to save!"

The prophet continues with words that contain revelatory importance to understand why I believe and am declaring that we are in a season of *victory*:

DEFEATING THE SPIRIT OF HYENA

> Why are your clothes so red, as if you have been treading out grapes?

Bozrah was the capital city of the ancient country of Edom, which is the most rebuked, most castigated and judged country in the Old Testament. Think about that statement. It should stand out to us because I would've thought the Babylonians or the Philistines would've had that badge. But it's Edom … including its leaders and government.

What is it about Edom that would give them the infamous title of "the most rebuked"? That's not the trophy you want to take home or a badge you post on Facebook: "Hi, I'm the most rebuked country in the history of the Old Testament." What is it about them? After searching the Scriptures, I found the answer. The reason Edom is the most rebuked country in the Bible is because they attacked Israel when they were down.

Israel had just been attacked and was suffering from a devastating loss at the hands of the Babylonians. They had been decimated as a people. Their land stolen, their future children—their Shadrachs, Meshachs, Abednagos, and Daniels—had been taken off into captivity. And when they were already down, Edom came and kicked them again. They plundered the plundered and wounded the wounded.

Just when Israel thought it couldn't get any worse,

The reason Edom is the most rebuked country in the Bible is because they attacked Israel when they were down.

Edom came and said, "Oh yes it can." And God saw. (See Ezekiel 25:12–14 and Jeremiah 49:7–22 for God's prophecies against Edom.)

Do you remember play areas at the mall or restaurants? Maybe you've been a parent watching your kids play when out of nowhere a kid shows up and things start to get a bit rough. You sit back and try not to get involved because you know your child has to learn to be kind and learn how to handle a difficult person. You watch him or her trip and fall or interact with others and you don't react (even if you really want to) because you're trying not to be "that parent." But when a kid pushes, kicks, or starts to bully your kid, something stirs in your spirit and you rise up to put a stop to the nonsense. I've been known to step into a ball pit at Chuck E. Cheese entertainment center and restaurant—I mean I'm crawling right in there to defend and protect my kids!

Well, that's what God did. He saw His kids struggling. He saw His kids being attacked. He saw what they were going through. And when Edom came and kicked them when they were already down, the Father spoke up and said, "NO MORE!" No more kicking my kids. No more decimation! God said ENOUGH!

Chapter 3

MOCKERS AND THIEVES

I was in Nebraska preaching at Lord of Hosts Church when God originally spoke to me about this ruling spirit of Edom and that it is the ruling spirit of the age we're living in. God said to me, "Tony, that is the spirit of hyena."

I asked the Lord, "What does that mean?" God started downloading, and I started writing. He said, "This is the spirit of hyena. Hyenas don't kill; hyenas steal. Hyenas are mockers and thieves that take possession of things that don't belong to them. Hyenas don't want to fight, they don't want to work, they don't want to hunt. They just want to pester; they mock and ridicule."

This is the spirit that is attacking the church right now. Hyenas pester, mock, and antagonize lions specifically. They let lions do the hunting and the killing, and then hyenas swoop in to steal what the lions have worked for.

Hyenas taunt lions with the hopes of distracting them from their kill. Distraction is key to thievery. If you take your eyes off of your prize, then a hyena will sneak in and plunder what you worked for. Even their laughter and mockery is to cause distraction. Science tells us that hyenas are led by "alpha females." To maintain power, the alpha females resort to infanticide and kill the majority of their young. For some reason, these alpha females think to maintain power and authority and social status in the pack, they have to kill their young. And so, they do it by crushing the skulls of baby hyenas.

These alpha females also hate males. To them, males are fools. A male only serves one purpose: procreation. The alpha-female hyenas will make males work to get to impregnate a female but then kick them out of the pride, thereby emasculating them.

It's important to note that for thousands of years it was thought that hyenas were genderless. It wasn't until the last few centuries that experts discovered that there are in fact both male and female hyenas, debunking thousands of years of classifying them as "genderless." Hyenas communicate to each other through that laughter. Their mockery communicates how close they are to

Hyenas don't kill; hyenas steal. Hyenas are mockers and thieves that take possession of things that don't belong to them.

plunder. Their laughter is annoying and distracting but serves the two-fold purpose: to communicate to their posse how close they are to death or plunder, and to distract lions.

Hyenas cannot do lions any harm, unless the lion is injured and roams off and gets alone. And even at that, one hyena cannot bring down one lion. One hyena will need to get other hyenas, and then they'll attack all at once to bring down the injured or lonely lion.

Now that I've just described to you what hyenas do in nature, allow me to flip it and talk about the spirit of hyena. The spirit of hyena is pestering, mocking, and antagonizing the Spirit-filled church today. This spirit wants our crowds, our money, our buildings and property, and it wants our authority, but it doesn't want to have to pray for it, fast for it, or intercede for it. It doesn't want to live in consecration to God for it. The spirit of hyena just wants to swoop in and steal what their father's generation paid a price for. It has infected and overwhelmed the church's offspring, I'm sad to say.

They want to live off of the residue of their grandfather's prayer life. They want to live off of the residual of the blessings from their mothers and fathers who prayed and fasted and called things as though they were even when they were not. Then after stealing the blessing, they get into pulpits and act like they don't even know what Pentecost is. The spirit of hyena is behind this robbery.

MOCKERS AND THIEVES

This spirit taunts the Pentecostal church and those who move in the charismatic gifts and power of the Spirit. They make mockery of the holy things of God. I understand if the world mocks us because they don't understand. But I'm concerned about the spirit of hyena in the church.

Mocking people who can no longer stand because they are overpowered by the Spirit of God.

Making fun of people speaking in other tongues.

Ridiculing the manifestations of the Holy Spirit.

Scoffing at the praise, exuberance, and demonstrations of faith of the people of God, including demonstrative acts of praise and worship—as if restoration, salvation, healing, blessing, and abundance are not worth getting excited about!

A deceptive spirit justifies dancing and getting excited over making a little bit of money day trading, yet acts as if the church is weird! This spirit of hyena makes a mockery of what God calls holy.

I think it hurts the heart of God to see how the children of yesteryear's revivals have allowed the spirit of hyena to dominate them. I'm talking about church kids who know better. They were raised in revival. They were baptized in the Spirit. They know the fire of God I'm talking about. They would not be where they are today without the love of God and the power of the Holy Spirit. But now they act like the works of the Spirit

This spirit taunts the Pentecostal church and those who move in the charismatic gifts and power of the Spirit.

are foreign. They have been given over to another spirit, but I call it out by name. It's the spirit of hyena, and I rebuke it in the name of Jesus!

The spirit of hyena is also seeking to erase gender lines and distinctions and not recognize male and female. As I said earlier, hyenas were once thought to be genderless because of how identical their bodeies are. This spirit of erasing or ignoring gender has been around a long time, but today more than ever it is attempting to usurp authority over this generation where there's no longer male, there's no longer female, there's no he, there's no her, there's no him, there's no she. That's the spirit of hyena, and I call you out by name and I rebuke you from this land in the name of Jesus of Nazareth!

Hyenas kill their young to maintain their manipulative grip of power of the pack, as well as to regulate the population of their packs. This is the spirit of abortion and murder that has infected our nation as well as other nations such as China (through population control) for decades, but I call an end to it in the name of Jesus of Nazareth!

The spirit of hyena promotes and celebrates abortion and infanticide. I believe this spirit has influenced wicked rulers in our land—including governors, representatives, senators, and delegates—who said it was okay to murder a baby if a baby was born after a botched abortion. That is infanticide. This is murder, and again, it's the spirit of hyena. But I take authority over it and I rebuke it in the name of Jesus!

I've heard hyenas laughing for the last few months. I can hear them in the background, in moments when I'm alone.

I can hear them laughing at and in the Oval Office.

I can hear them laughing in the Capitol Building.

I can hear them from state capitals and municipalities.

I hear them laughing on Facebook, I hear them laughing on Instagram.

I hear them making a mockery, but I heard the Lion of the tribe of Judah roar and say, "ENOUGH!"

Chapter 4

KICK THAT DEVIL OUT

If you want to win a fight, you have to know what you're fighting—you have to understand the enemy. The Bible says Lucifer is the king of the kingdom of darkness. He's not effective if you know he's there. He operates in the shadows and in the darkness. That's why sickness comes and you are confused why you're not feeling well. Marital or parenting problems come and you wonder what's happening—because you don't know what's lurking in the shadows.

When the kingdom of darkness suspects that you're about to have victory, it resorts to one of its best tactics: fear through intimidation. But this kind of intimidation is from the shadows. The enemy doesn't want you to know he's there or what you're fighting against. What's in the shadows appears bigger than it actually is.

If you want to win a fight, you have to know what you're fighting—you have to understand the enemy.

This is how the spirit of hyena works. But it is written: resist the devil and he *shall* flee (see James 4:7). When the enemy steps out of the shadows and exposes himself, and you resist him, the Bible says he can't stand there any longer. He shall flee. I believe the church of the living God, through the authority of the name of Jesus and the power of the Holy Spirit, is positioned to cause this spirit to flee!

We are the sons and the daughters of the Lion of the tribe of Judah. When it comes to us lions, hyenas can't do us any harm as long as we're united. As long as we're together, the spirit of hyena can't hurt us. In fact, it won't even attack us. It'll mock us, it'll laugh at us, but it won't dare attack us.

But when you break unity for agenda, denominationalism, race, and culture, causing people to go their own ways, then we leave ourselves susceptible to a nasty old hyena that will come and attack us. But even at that, the hyena will not attack unless it sees that you're wounded and down. It's when you're in depression, when you're all alone, the hyena will think, *Now!* The hyena will consider attacking an injured lion. But even when the lion is injured, the hyena knows, *Nope, I can't do it alone. I don't possess enough strength and power alone.* So, it'll go and find more hyenas to help in the attack. Do you see how the spiritual mirrors the natural?

DEFEATING THE SPIRIT OF HYENA

Matthew 12:43–45 (NKJV) records this warning of Jesus:

> "When an unclean spirit goes out of a man, he goes through dry places, seeking rest, and finds none. Then he says, 'I will return to my house from which I came.' And when he comes, he finds it empty, swept, and put in order. Then he goes and takes with him seven other spirits more wicked than himself, and they enter and dwell there; and the last state of that man is worse than the first."

When an evil spirit leaves someone, it seeks a new place where it can dwell. When it finds nowhere else to rest, the evil spirit returns to where it once was. That ought to upset you. That ought to stir anger in you that an evil spirit—from which Christ has set you free—says, "I will return to my house."

How about you put the enemy in his place: "Devil, this is not your house! This is the temple of the Holy Ghost!" You ought to walk up and down your house, past the bedrooms of your children, and say, "Suicide, perversion, rebellion, this is not your house! Poverty, this is not your house! This is the temple of the Holy Ghost."

The evil spirit says, "I'll go back to my house," but it finds "its house" clean and swept. No residue. No

The church of the living God, through the authority of the name of Jesus and the power of the Holy Spirit, is positioned to cause this spirit to flee!

evidence of what used to be. The spirit comes back and says, "Where's that perversion I left? Where's that fighting spirit I left between that husband and that wife? Where's that cutting spirit that was on their kids? I know I left something here that would lead that kid to commit suicide. Where did it go? This doesn't look the way it used to look. They don't talk the way they used to talk. They don't walk the way they used to walk. They don't even decorate the house the way they used to decorate. They don't go to the same websites. What happened to my house?" And I think that at that moment the spirit of hyena hears from heaven, "It's because it was never your house to begin with."

Every generation struggles with thoughts of *I'm not going to make it, I can't live for God, I can't do this.* You're not the only one who has struggled with thoughts that you're the only one who battles with sin, addiction, or *that thing.* It is the spirit of hyena that whispers from the shadows that you're the only one going through this. It convinces you that you're a liar, a hypocrite, and that there's no reason to try to live for God. I call that spirit out today by name and I rebuke it in the name of Jesus! As for me and my house, we will serve the Lord! For this promise is unto you and unto your children, and unto your children's children. And yes, even those that are far off.

The Bible says the evil spirit finds it clean and swept, and do you know what the spirit of hyena does? It goes and it finds seven more spirits. Just like a hyena who is going to attack but then goes and gets seven more hyenas. That's how the spirit of hyena attacks the injured lions of God. This spirit says, "Let me get seven more sins, seven more vices, seven more spirits of depression, loneliness, and insecurity. Let me get seven of my best friends and then let's go and attack."

Children of God, take notice. If the enemy is coming at you seven times stronger than he used to, it's because your enemy recognizes you're seven times stronger than you used to be. He recognizes there's something different about you. Your enemy recognizes that the One in you is greater than any attacking foe.

I've mentioned how hyenas steal and are cunning in their thievery. Hyenas are also mockers. Their laugh is annoying and distracting. But did you know their laughter is not just noise? It is communication. Hyenas make laughing noises when they're close to stealing what belongs to a lion.

Do you see the spiritual parallel? Hyena spirits laugh when they think they're about to get your kids. They mock when they think you and your spouse are close to a divorce or they think they are close to stealing your business. There's a sound of mockery when the hyena thinks he's close to stealing your salvation. But do you know what scares off the hyena? You know what makes the hyena stop laughing?

Do you know what scares off the hyena? You know what makes the hyena stop laughing? One lion's roar. The One in you is greater than any attacking foe.

One lion's roar.

By the authority of God, I speak to the spirit of hyena and I tell you the Lion of the tribe of Judah is about to roar!

We are one lion's roar away from the mouth of the Lion of the tribe of Judah from getting our government back, our children back, our economy back, and our churches back.

So, I say to you oh great King of Judah:

Roar!

Roar!

Roar!

If the devil—the spirit of hyena—thinks he's the only one that can laugh, allow me to remind you what is written in Job 5:22, 24 says to the people of God: we'll laugh in the face of distraction, and we'll laugh in the face of famine!

> You shall laugh at destruction and famine, and you shall not be afraid of the beasts of the earth. You shall know that your tent is in peace; you shall visit your dwelling and find nothing amiss.

Spirit of hyena, I know you tried to steal, I know you tried to plunder, I know you tried to attack, but we foiled your attack and now we laugh at you. Ha! You tried but you lost. Ha, ha, ha! God is faithful! And every demon is cursed!

You want to really tick off hell? If you've been through anything in the last twelve months, if you've had to ward off any demons, if you've had to fight anything off, if you've had all of hell rise up against you and you really want to send the devil back to the pit from whence he came? Laugh at him! Laugh in his direction! Remember, don't look up; look down, because he's under your feet!

Chapter 5

HOW GOD FIGHTS FOR YOU

Isaiah 63 tells us that out of Edom (the land of hyenas) came One. And when the prophets saw Him, they asked, "Who is this, that cometh from Edom? Out of the land of destruction. Traveling in strength? Who is this? Whose garments are stained bloody red. And a voice sounded, it is I!"

Out of grief, out of death, out of sorrow, out of rebellion comes One. He's coming out, and His garments are stained red. The prophet asks, "Who is it?" Who is this person that can be stained, dirtied, and bloodied yet look glorious at the same time? This reminds me of Psalm 24:7–8:

Lift up your heads, O you gates!
And be lifted up, you everlasting doors!

> And the King of glory shall come in.
> Who is this King of glory?
> The Lord strong and mighty,
> The Lord mighty in battle.

When the psalmist asks, "Who is this King of glory?" the Lord responds, "It is I the Lord, strong and mighty, the Lord mighty in battle."

The Lord told Isaiah the prophet, "I am the One who speaks in righteousness, who is mighty to save." Can you see the word picture? He is bloody, He is dirty, He is stained, and there's a scowl on His face. This isn't a sweet Precious Moments baby Jesus from your manger scene. Jesus is coming out of a place of destruction, out of a place of desolation. He is bloodied, He is stained, and He has vengeance in His heart. Jesus is not happy, because He's seen His children's oppression, their suffering and afflictions. He's seen how the enemies of hell have risen up against His Bride, and He can take it no longer.

I prophesy to this nation and to the nations of the world that this next manifestation of God is not God coming as the Prince of Peace. He's not coming as Joy unspeakable and full of glory. He's not coming as the Wonderful Counselor. He's coming as Exodus 15:3 (KJV) describes Him:

> The Lord is a warrior; Yahweh is his name!

Jesus has seen His children's oppression, their suffering and afflictions. He's seen how the enemies of hell have risen up against His Bride, and He can take it no longer.

He's coming as the warrior God. He's coming as a battle ax. He's coming as the mighty God. The Lord that is strong in battle. He has seen families broken up, children running away, money being stolen, houses falling apart, depression and anxiety driving people into a pit, and He can stand it no longer! The Lion of the tribe of Judah roars and says, "Enough!"

He is coming from a fight. Have you ever seen someone come from a real fight? If you come out of a fight and your hair is still combed, you didn't really fight. If you come out and your clothes are still tucked in, you didn't fight. But when you have holes in your clothes, your shirt has been stretched and torn, and your hair has flipped the other direction and you're missing a tooth, then you know something really went down!

The Lion of the tribe of Judah is coming out of your depression, out of your fight, out of your children's rebellion, out of desolation. He's coming out of everything that's been hindering your walk with God. He's coming out and there are stains, nail prints, and blood. He bears our iniquities. The punishment that brought us peace was upon Him, and by His stripes we are healed of all that ails us—emotionally, mentally, physically, and spiritually.

Isaiah 53:5 (NLT) says,

> But he was pierced for our rebellion, crushed for our sins.

He was beaten so we could be whole.
He was whipped so we could be healed.

I see the image of the Warrior coming out with bloodied garments, knowing that it is the Lion of the tribe of Judah. Read this passage from Isaiah 63:3–5, which tells us *why* the Warrior's clothes are so red with blood:

> "I have been treading the winepress alone;
> no one was there to help me.
> In my anger I have trampled my enemies
> as if they were grapes.
> In my fury I have trampled my foes.
> Their blood has stained my clothes.
> For the time has come for me to avenge
>   my people,
> to ransom them from their oppressors.
> I was amazed to see that no one intervened
> to help the oppressed.
> So I myself stepped in to save them with my
>   strong arm,
> and my wrath sustained me."

The Bible says God looked for someone to fight with Him but couldn't find anyone. He was looking for some prophets and some pastors, some bishops and

This next battle that I win, you won't be able to say it was Republicans or Democrats. It wasn't a man, it wasn't a woman, it wasn't a group of people. It was the Lion of the tribe of Judah!

evangelists, some saints and some worshippers. He was looking for some Christians that would fight the battle, but He couldn't find anyone. But hear the Word of the Lord. He said, "I made up my mind. I'll fight this one all by myself."

This next victory that's coming to us, no denomination will be able to take credit for it. No singular man or woman will be able to take credit for it. The Lion of the tribe of Judah says, "I'm going to fight and I'm going to win this one all by myself. Because I share my glory with no other man or woman."

The Spirit of God says, "I'm still a jealous God, and I'm hearing you say other people's names more than you say my name. I hear you say *Donald Trump* more than you say *Jesus*. You're saying *Joe Biden* more than you're saying *Jesus*. You say *Kamala* and *Nancy* more than you say *Jesus*, but there is no power in those names.

"But there is a name that's above every other name. And one day every knee shall bow, and every tongue shall confess, Jesus Christ is Lord to the glory of God the Father. So, God says, This next battle that I win, you won't be able to say it was Republicans or Democrats. It wasn't a man, it wasn't a woman, it wasn't a group of people. It was the Lion of the tribe of Judah! I'm restoring all glory and honor to my name! You will know that your victory is in me and me alone!"

I see this bloodied Warrior walking toward me and

the Pentecostal in me says, "Thank God for the blood." I'm thinking it's the blood that washes white as snow. I'm thinking it's the blood of Calvary; it's the blood of my Savior. But then the Lord speaks and says, "Wrong blood." He says, "You can shout over it and dance over it. But you need to know whose blood this is. This is not the blood for the propitiation of your sins. I carry on me the stains of the blood of your enemy because I didn't just go fight the battle, I won the battle and I bring you evidence that the enemy is defeated. If you could see in the heavenlies today, there is One coming out of Edom and He is bringing you the evidence that I have won the victory: the blood of your enemies!"

God Fights for You

I can think of no better way to explain how God defends you than recollecting what I call "The Parable of Taco Bell."

When I was an adolescent, my school held a special meeting for students and parents to warn us of a dangerous location they felt students should avoid: a Taco Bell that was in the middle of gang territory. It was known that gangs had pretty much taken over the parking lot. The police officer leading the meeting admonished us to avoid that location at all cost. They warned both students and parents.

Being the tough know-it-all kid I was, I thought I was immune to the admonishment and I could venture to Taco Bell with no issue. So, one random afternoon my friend and I got on our bicycles and took off to Taco Bell. Upon arriving in the parking lot, we were met by three tall guys who looked like Goliath's younger brothers to me. They surrounded my friend and me and said, "Get off your bikes." Within moments they were the new owners of our bicycles.

I walked home ashamed and upset my bicycle had been stolen, nervous about telling my mother, and simultaneously praying for the rapture to occur so I wouldn't have to tell her.

As I got closer to the house, I could see that my mom was sitting on the porch. The closer I got, the higher I could see her eyebrows raised, sensing something was up. When I finally reached the porch, she asked me where my bike was. I explained that I had gone to Taco Bell and it had been stolen from me.

There was a moment of awkward silence and then heavy breathing. I knew she was furious, but she had yet to utter a word. Then she said, "Get in the car." I asked her where we were going and she said, "Taco Bell."

The trip from my childhood home to that Taco Bell, in a car, took no longer than three minutes, but if felt like we were on a long road trip. I prayed and prayed. I was pleading to Jesus for His help for whatever my mom was about to do, and also pleading the blood for me because I knew I was in trouble.

Can you hear your heavenly Father say these words to your enemy today? "NO ONE takes what belongs to my kids!"

When we arrived in the parking lot, sure enough, those boys were still there and they were riding my bicycle. My mother quickly parked the car, whipped the door open, and marched toward those boys. She yelled, "HEY! THAT'S OUR BIKE!" The boys started laughing at my mom. I guess I should've warned them. You never laugh at my mom.

My mother said, "I TOLD YOU THAT'S OUR BIKE," and with that she pushed the boys down to the ground, grabbed the bike, and marched back to the vehicle. She put the bike in the trunk and started back home. Then looking at me in the rearview mirror, she said, "NO ONE steals what belongs to my kids."

Can you hear your heavenly Father say these words to your enemy today? "NO ONE takes what belongs to my kids!"

I want to put the devil and his spirit of hyena on notice today: My heavenly Father is coming from heaven, like an angry mama headed to Taco Bell to get her son's bike back! My heavenly Father is coming to get back EVERYTHING the enemy has stolen!

So, what can you do if you've been attacked by the spirit of mockery and thievery, the spirit of hyena?

DEFEATING THE SPIRIT OF HYENA

1. Know who you belong to. You are a child of the Creator and Savior of the universe.
2. Acknowledge you need God's help. Have you felt like you need to do everything yourself? God wants to fight this battle with you and for you. He will do the heavy lifting. Your role is to trust Him.
3. Come *boldly* before the throne of grace and ask God for His help. Do not be afraid, and don't let shame or condemnation keep you from the help the Holy Spirit wants to provide.
4. Cast your cares upon the Lord. Tell Him all your fears and frustrations and trust that He will come to your defense. The Bible says that as you wait upon the Lord He will renew your strength.
5. Know without question that God saw the attack and says, "Enough is enough!" Declare and pray the Victory Scriptures on the following pages to align your heart and mind with the will and Word of God.

Pray with me: *Father God, thank you for the privilege of being a part of your family. Thank you for loving me! Thank you for standing up for me! Thank you for defending me! I need your help with _____ (share your heart with the Lord). I've done what I can do. I've tried what I can try. I need you, God, to do what only you can do, in Jesus's name!*

Church, I'm more excited than I have ever been—to be alive "for such a time as this." The ancient prophecies of revival are coming to pass in our day. It would've been better for the enemy to leave us alone. He shouldn't have messed with us. He's provoked the wrath of God and the passion of the people of God. We're getting up! We're getting our authority, our voice, our zeal, our passion back! We're taking our marriages, families, schools, colleges, and nations back for the glory of Christ.

The hyenas are whimpering in defeat because the Lion has roared!

35 VICTORY SCRIPTURES

Exodus 14:14 ESV "The Lord will fight for you, and you have only to be silent."

Exodus 15:6 ESV "Your right hand, O Lord, glorious in power, your right hand, O Lord, shatters the enemy."

Deuteronomy 9:3 ESV "Know therefore today that he who goes over before you as a consuming fire is the Lord your God. He will destroy them and subdue them before you. So you shall drive them out and make them perish quickly, as the Lord has promised you."

For the Lord your God is the one who goes with you to fight for you against your enemies to give you victory. – Deuteronomy 20:4 NIV

Deuteronomy 33:27 ESV The eternal God is your dwelling place, and underneath are the everlasting arms. And he thrust out the enemy before you and said, Destroy.

1 Samuel 2:9 ESV "He will guard the feet of his faithful ones."

DEFEATING THE SPIRIT OF HYENA

2 Samuel 22:2 ESV "The Lord is my rock and my fortress and my deliverer."

Psalms 20:6 NIV The Lord gives victory to His anointed.

Psalms 21:5 NIV Through the victories you gave, his glory is great; you have bestowed on him splendor and majesty.

Psalm 34:17 ESV When the righteous cry for help, the Lord hears and delivers them out of all their troubles.

Psalm 37:39 ESV The salvation of the righteous is from the Lord; he is their stronghold in the time of trouble.

Psalm 44:5 ESV Through you we push down our foes; through your name we tread down those who rise up against us.

Psalms 44:7 ESV But you have saved us from our foes and have put to shame those who hate us.

35 VICTORY SCRIPTURES

Psalm 46:1 ESV God is our refuge and strength, a very present help in trouble.

Psalm 60:12 NLT With God's help we will do mighty things, for he will trample down our foes.

Psalm 62:1 ESV For God alone my soul waits in silence; from him comes my salvation.

Psalm 138:7 ESV Though I walk in the midst of trouble, you preserve my life; you stretch out your hand against the wrath of my enemies, and your right hand delivers me.

Isaiah 41:11 ESV Behold, all who are incensed against you shall be put to shame and confounded; those who strive against you shall be as nothing and shall perish.

Isaiah 43:2 NLT "When you go through deep waters, I will be with you. When you go through rivers of difficulty, you will not drown. When you walk through the fire of oppression, you will not be burned up; the flames will not consume you."

DEFEATING THE SPIRIT OF HYENA

Isaiah 54:17 ESV "No weapon that is fashioned against you shall succeed, and you shall confute every tongue that rises against you in judgment. This is the heritage of the servants of the Lord and their vindication from me, declares the Lord."

Isaiah 61:7 ESV Instead of your shame there shall be a double portion; instead of dishonor they shall rejoice in their lot; therefore in their land they shall possess a double portion; they shall have everlasting joy.

Jeremiah 1:8 ESV "Do not be afraid of them, for I am with you to deliver you, declares the Lord."

Zechariah 9:12 ESV Return to your stronghold, O prisoners of hope; today I declare that I will restore to you double.

Luke 10:19 NIV "Behold, I have given you authority to tread on serpents and scorpions, and over all the power of the enemy, and nothing shall hurt you."

35 VICTORY SCRIPTURES

John 1:5 NIV The light shines in the darkness, and the darkness has not overcome it.

John 10:10 ESV "The thief comes only to steal and kill and destroy. I came that they may have life and have it abundantly."

John 16:33, NIV "I have said these things to you, that in me you may have peace. In the world you will have tribulation. But take heart; I have overcome the world."

1 Corinthians 10:13 NIV No temptation has overtaken you except what is common to mankind. And God is faithful; He will not let you be tempted beyond what you can bear. But when you are tempted, He will also provide a way out so that you can endure it.

1 Corinthians 15:57 NIV But thanks be to God! He gives us the victory through our Lord Jesus Christ.

2 Corinthians 2:14 NIV But thanks be to God, who in Christ always leads us in triumphal procession, and through us spreads the fragrance of the knowledge of him everywhere.

DEFEATING THE SPIRIT OF HYENA

Philippians 4:13 NLT For I can do everything through Christ, who gives me strength.

2 Timothy 4:18 ESV The Lord will rescue me from every evil deed and bring me safely into his heavenly kingdom. To him be the glory forever and ever. Amen.

1 John 4:4 NIV You, dear children, are from God and have overcome them, because the one who is in you is greater than the one who is in the world.

1 John 5:4 NIV For everyone born of God overcomes the world. This is the victory that has overcome the world, even our faith.

Revelation 21:3–7 NLT I heard a loud shout from the throne, saying, "Look, God's home is now among his people! He will live with them, and they will be his people. God himself will be with them. He will wipe every tear from their eyes, and there will be no more death or sorrow or crying or pain. All these things are gone forever." And the one sitting on the throne said, "Look, I am making everything new!" And then he said to me, "Write this down, for what I tell you is trustworthy and true." And he also said, "It is finished! I am the Alpha and the Omega—the Beginning and the End. To all who are thirsty I will give freely from the springs of the water of life. All who are victorious will inherit all these blessings, and I will be their God, and they will be my children.

ABOUT THE AUTHOR

Tony Suárez is the founder of Revivalmakers, a Spirit-filled evangelistic ministry that travels from church to church and also hosts events, tent revivals, healing services, and crusades around the world. A third-generation Pentecostal preacher, Tony's greatest passion in life is preaching and teaching about Jesus and watching God save and heal. His calling is to be a remnant of Pentecost to the world.

He is a regular host and guest on TBN and the Victory Channel. His preaching ministry and program Revivalmakers can be found daily on various Christian outlets.

Along with *Defeating the Spirit of Hyena*, Tony has also written:

Use Me Lord (2012)
The Triumphant Church (2018)
REVIVALMAKERS (May 2022)

In addition to his ministry work, Tony serves as the Chief Operating Officer of the National Hispanic

Christian Leadership Conference (NHCLC), the nation's largest Hispanic Christian organization, serving more than 40,000 congregations in the United States as well as thousands of churches abroad. Through his role as COO, Pastor Tony regularly meets with members of Congress and the White House, and speaks at events to advance the cause of righteousness, life, and religious liberty.

Tony and his wife, Jina, along with their five children, reside in Tennessee.

Facebook and Instagram:
@pastortonysuarez

Website: www.tonysuarez.com

YouTube: revivalmakersTV